T0380917

The Most High

Holy Quran (Chapter 87) Workbook

Fadwa Amin Zagzoug

To order additional copies of this book, contact:
Xlibris
844-714-8691
www.Xlibris.com
Orders@Xlibris.com

ISBN: Softcover   979-8-3694-1445-3
            Hardcover   979-8-3694-1446-0
            EBook   979-8-3694-1444-6

Print information available on the last page

Rev. date: 01/08/2024

Contents

Introduction

Vocabulary worksheets

Board Game Challenge

Acknowledgments

I am forever thankful and grateful towards my only creator and beloved, Allah (الله). I am thankful because Allah inspired me to have this quality to begin with.

I am also thankful for all God's prophets and messengers (الأنبياء والرُسُل) especially the last prophet and the prophet of Islam Muhammad peace and blessings be upon him (PBUH).

(رسول الله محمد بن عبد الله صلى الله عليه وسلم تسليما كثيراً)

Prophets and messengers pass knowledge to us from God and have endured great hardship in their path. They are our role models and for them I am forever thankful and grateful.

Abu Huraira reported: Prophet Muhammad (PBUH), said:

" Whoever does not thank people has not thanked Allah."

عَن أَبي هُريرة رضي الله عنه قال: قال رسول الله صلى الله عليه وسَلَّم: " من لا يَشكِر الناس لا يَشكُر الله "

حَديث صَحيح- سُنن الترمذي .

All through my life, God All Mighty put people in my path that are kind, knowledgeable, giving, and sometimes of deep faith. The first people that come to mind are my parents, husband, grandparents, family, and friends. My teachers are one of my greatest blessings as well since that they always inspired me to do my best and dealt with my short comings with great patience and love. I also extend my special thanks and gratitude to Shaykha Ebtsam Fawzy who reviewed this workbook for accuracy and correctness. Shaykha Ebtsam is Hafiza of the Holy Quran and holds an Ijazah in the Qira'a of Asem. She is also certified in memorizing the Holy Quran with Hafs narration from Al-Sunnah AL Muhammadiyah institute cooperated with AL-Azhar. Shaykha Ebtsam is currently teaching online classes through Jannat Al Quran website (https://www.jannatalquran.com). Her experience with teaching Quran to non-Arabic native speakers has made this workbook a valuable resource to both learners and teachers of the Holy Quran. In addition, my special thanks go to Nesma Abdelrahman for the wonderful graphic design she did on this workbook. I really appreciate her patience and the hard work she did to make the workbook look so professional and appealing to the reader.

How to use this workbook?

(Summary Chart)

Step 1
Listen
to verses professional recitation (Example: Mahmoud Al-Hussary recitation)

Step 2
Learn meaning
by reading English translation (Example: QuranEnc.com)

Step 3
Do worksheets
one section at a time

Step 4
Recite
section from workbook or from memory

Step 5
Repeat
with a new section until entire chapter is complete

Step 6
Play
the board game to review the entire chapter

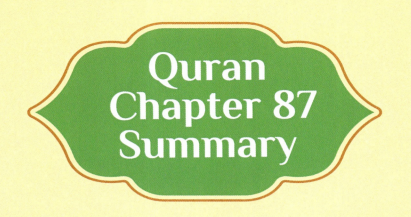

Quran Chapter 87 Summary

مُلَخَّص سُورَةِ الأَعْلَى

After learning this chapter and understanding it's simple meanings the learner would realize that the theme of the chapter is the facade of this world. God Almighty describes to us how the new and lush green pasture soon changes to a dark and withered chaff. He reminds us that this life is temporary just as the green pasture is temporary. Allah is so merciful and loving that he sent us Prophet Muhammad (PBUH) to remind us about this truth.

God Almighty also talks about the fact that there are two groups of people when it comes to the reminders. The first group will make use of the reminders because their hearts are in constant remembrance of the Most high- Allah. However, the second group will not make use of the reminders because their hearts are in constant quest of the façade of this world. They are too distracted to realize that there is more than meets the eye. The chapter then clearly states the fate of the first group and the fate of the second group in the hereafter. Again, Allah is so merciful and loving that he lists the actions that are going to save all of us from the façade of this world.

Allah (سُبْحَانَهُ وَتَعَالَى) has created us and the people who came before us as well- the people of prophet Ibrahim and Musa peace and blessings be upon both of them. Therefore, Allah knows all of us humans best and states that we prefer this world and its pleasures. Nevertheless, he teaches all of us that the hereafter is better and more lasting than this temporary worldly life. In many verses of the Quran, Allah promised to preserve his word- the Quran until the end of time. In this chapter of the Holy Quran Allah All Mighty gives assurance to our prophet Muhammad (PBUH) that this message will be forever preserved through the Holy Quran. He also reminds us that this message is not knew as it was revealed to other prophets before Muhammad (PBUH). This lesson will also help the people that will come after us until the end of time.

Recognize
Arabic
vocabulary

Listen to
Correct
Recitation

The Learning Styles & Memorizing the Holy Quran

Say
Correct
Recitation

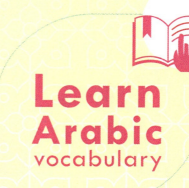

Learn
Arabic
vocabulary

﴿ وَلَقَد يَسَّرْنَا الْقُرْءَانَ لِلذِّكْرِ فَهَلْ مِن مُّدَّكِرٍ ﴾

سورة القمر آيه رقم ١٧

And We have indeed made the Quran easy to understand and remember ,
then is there any that will remember?

سُورَةُ الأَعْلَى

Surat Al-A 'la

Chapter 87

Vocabulary Worksheets

بِسْمِ اللهِ الرَّحْمَنِ الرَّحِيمِ

سَبِّحِ آسْمَ رَبِّكَ ٱلْأَعْلَى (1) ٱلَّذِي خَلَقَ فَسَوَّىٰ (2) وَٱلَّذِي قَدَّرَ فَهَدَىٰ (3) وَٱلَّذِيَ أَخْرَجَ ٱلْمَرْعَىٰ (4) فَجَعَلَهُ غُثَآءً أَحْوَىٰ (5)....

Glorify the name of your Lord, the Most High (1) Who created and fashioned in due proportion (2) and Who determined [the creation] then inspired them (3) and Who brings forth the pasture (4) then makes it into withered chaff (5)...

Color & then copy the words

سَبِّحِ اسْمَ رَبِّكَ

(Glorify the name of your lord)

_____ 5

_____ 1

_____ 6

_____ 2

_____ 7

_____ 3

_____ 8

_____ 4

The Most High _____

الْأَعْـلَى

(The Most High)

I. Copy

----------------- 1

----------------- 2

----------------- 3

----------------- 4

----------------- 5

II. This is one of God's 99 names
Reflect on what it means to you.

Some Humans display qualities such as knowledge and mercy.
However, God All Mighty is the most high in displaying these same qualities.
Can you think of other qualities of God?
HINT: Review the 99 names of Allah.

All-Knowing
الْعَلِــيم

Most Compassionate
الــرَّؤُوف

1. ....

Almighty
الْعَــزِيز

5. ....

الْأَعْـلَـى
(The Most High)

2. ....

The Most Powerful
الْقَـدِير

Most Merciful
الــرَّحِيم

4. ....

The Ever Living
الْحَــي

3. ....

The Wise
الْحَكِيم

I. **Unscramble** the following words from verse one
and then **copy** the complete verse
five times on the lines provided below.

الْأَعْلَى / رَبِّكَ / سَبِّحِ / اسْمَ

(Glorify the name of your Lord, the Most High)

....1

....2

....3

....4

....5

II.   a) **Which vocabulary word above means (Glorify God) ?**

....

b) **Which vocabulary word above means (The most high) ?**

....

c) **Which vocabulary word above means (Your Lord) ?**

....

Vocabulary Word Work

Color the word

خَلَقَ

Recite the word

خَلَقَ

(Created)

Copy the word

```
_____3
```

```
_____1
```

```
_____4
```

```
_____2
```

Draw a picture of your favourite animal or plant

I. Read the following short paragraph.

God ALL Mighty Allah has created the universe and everything that is in it. However, there are four creations that God made with his own hands (as befitting to his Majesty). These are: his thrown (العرش), the pen (القلم), the Garden of Eden (جنة عدن), and our father Adam (PBUH) (آدَم عَليه الصَّلاةُ والسَّلام)

All of the other creations came to existence by Allah's supreme creative power of "Be, and it is". This concept has been mentioned in the Holly Quran eight times.

"Be, and it is" or Kun fa-yakun (كُن فَيَكُونُ) means that there is nothing greater than God's ability to create from nothingness (العَدَم). Allah also chooses the time for everything to happen as he pleases and with no boundaries as his ability cannot be compared to any of his creation.

Allah Almighty has created Adam with his hands to honor him and to elevate his position over the other creations such as nonliving things, plants and animals. God All Mighty has created nonliving things, plants, and animals to be of service to Adam and his offspring. Allah made Adam (PBUH) his deputy on Earth. Adam can perform his duties because Allah chose him and prepared him for this important task. Allah taught Adam all the knowledge that he needs to be the deputy on Earth and Allah gave him the ability to learn.

II. Answer the following questions:

1. List below what Allah (سُبحَانَهُ وَتَعَالى) has created with his own hands.

A)...

B)...

C)...

D)...

2. How did Allah (سُبحَانَهُ وَتَعَالى) create all of the other creations in the universe?

....

3. True or false:

a) There are no boundaries or limitations to God's ability to create anything at any time that he pleases.

b) Adam is the deputy of the Angels on Earth.

c) Not all creatures in this universe have a purpose.

4. How did Allah prepare Adam (PBUH) for his duties on Earth?

....

....

The Most High

I. Color and Copy

فَسَوَّىٰ

(Fashioned in due proportion)

-----------------------------------3

-----------------------------------1

-----------------------------------4

-----------------------------------2

II. Use the space below to reflect on your favorite flower beauty. Describe the colors, proportions, and parts symmetry . Think about how God All mighty has fashioned this simple creation in perfect proportions. **Draw a picture** of it below ....

I. Unscramble the following words from verse two
and then **copy** the complete verse
five times on the lines provided below.

الَّذِي/ فَ / خَلَقَ /سَوَّىٰ

(Who created and fashioned in due proportion)

1..

2..

3..

4..

5..

II.   **1- Which vocabulary word above means (Created) ?**

....

**2- Which vocabulary word above means
(Fashioned in due proportion) ?**

....

I. Color and Copy

فَهَدَىٰ

(Then inspired them)

قَدَّرَ

(Who determined
the creation)

```
----------------------------------1          ----------------------------------1

----------------------------------2          ----------------------------------2

----------------------------------3          ----------------------------------3
```

II. Copy the complete verse below

وَالَّذِي قَدَّرَ فَهَدَىٰ

```
.............................................. 1

.............................................. 2

.............................................. 3
```

verse number (3) worksheet (B)

I. Read the following short paragraph.

Many Scholars use the honeybees' and their colonies to explain verse three. This is because Allah has inspired (هَدَى أَو أَوْحَى) this amazing insect to build and live in complex colonies. Allah has created (خَلَقَ) the honeybees and inspired them to work together to maintain the hives and produce honey.

Allah determined (قَدَّرَ) three types of honeybees within every hive: workers, drones, and a queen. Each one of these types has a job that is predetermined by Allah. For example, the queen's only job is to lay eggs while the worker bees forage for nectar necessary to make the honey. In addition to making honey, worker honeybees have many other jobs among which are cleaning and ventilating the hive and feeding the larvae (baby bees). The drone's job is to mate with the queen. People of faith and reflection should learn from the honeybee to be obedient to Allah and to perform their duties. People should also learn to be sincere and hard working as the honeybees are.

Allah (سُبحانه وَ تَعَالَى) named an entire surah (سُورَةُ 16) in the Holy Quran after the honeybees. It is called Surat An-Nahl (سُورَةُ النَحْل). In verses 68 and 69 of this Surah Allah says:"

وَأَوْحَى رَبُّكَ إِلَى ٱلنَّحْلِ أَنِ ٱتَّخِذِي مِنَ ٱلْجِبَالِ بُيُوتًا وَمِنَ ٱلشَّجَرِ وَمِمَّا يَعْرِشُونَ (68) ثُمَّ كُلِي مِن كُلِّ ٱلثَّمَرَٰتِ فَٱسْلُكِي سُبُلَ رَبِّكِ ذُلُلًا يَخْرُجُ مِنْ بُطُونِهَا شَرَابٌ مُخْتَلِفٌ أَلْوَٰنُهُ فِيهِ شِفَاءٌ لِلنَّاسِ إِنَّ فِي ذَٰلِكَ لَآيَةً لِقَوْمٍ يَتَفَكَّرُونَ (69)

Your Lord inspired the bees, "Make homes in the mountains, the trees, and in the trellises that people put up (68) Then feed on every kind of fruit and follow the ways that your Lord made easy for you." There comes out from their bellies a drink of various colors, in which there is healing for people. Indeed, there is a sign in this for people who reflect (69)

II. Answer the following questions:

1. List the honeybee types below:

   A) ....

   B) ....

   C) ....

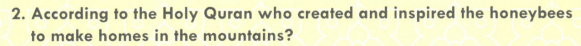

2. According to the Holy Quran who created and inspired the honeybees to make homes in the mountains?

   ....

3. What are some lessons that people can learn from the honeybees?

   ....

4. True or false:

   a) The job of the Queen and the drones is to make sure that all the worker bees stay on task.

   b) Honeybees live in complex colonies where an individual honeybee is not important for the well being or function of the entire colony.

   c) The word trellis means a frame of crossed bars used for support.

5. How did Allah describe the honey qualities in verse 69 (Surat An-Nahl) above?

   ....

Color and Copy

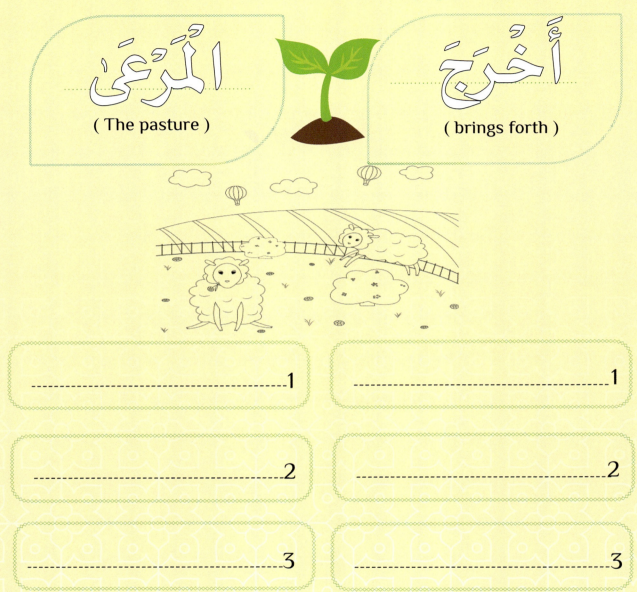

المَّرْعَى
(The pasture)

أَخْرَجَ
(brings forth)

1 -----------	1 -----------
2 -----------	2 -----------
3 -----------	3 -----------

II. Copy the complete verse below

وَالَّذِي أَخْرَجَ المَرْعَى

1 ....

2 ....

3 ....

I. Color and Copy

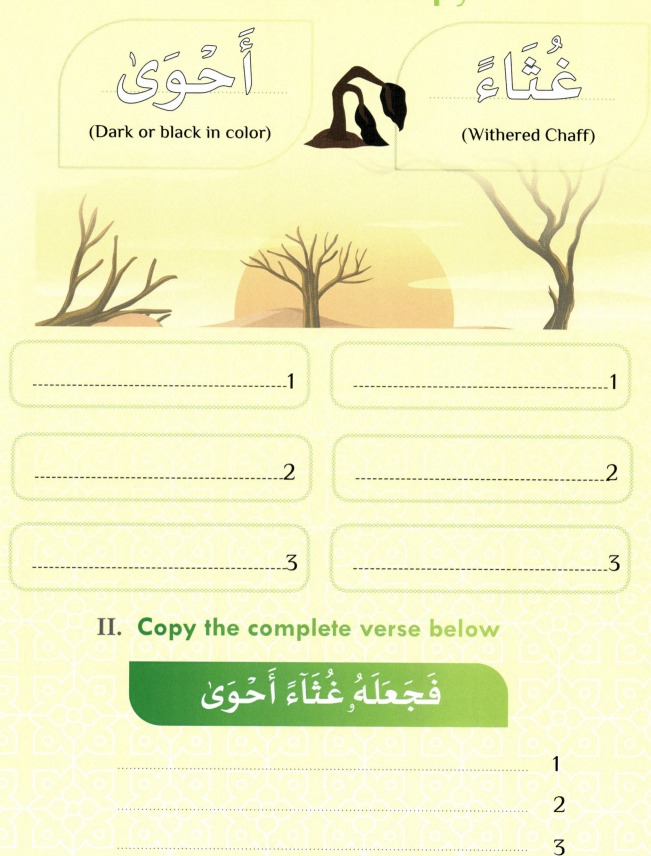

أَحْوَىٰ

(Dark or black in color)

غُثَاءً

(Withered Chaff)

--1

--1

--2

--2

--3

--3

II. Copy the complete verse below

فَجَعَلَهُ غُثَاءً أَحْوَىٰ

....1

....2

....3

Word Search!

Find each of the words in the box below.
Words may go across, down, up, or diagonally.

أَخْرَجَ	الأَعْلَى	سَبَّحَ	قَدَّرَ
أَحْوَى	خَلَقَ	المَرْعَى	فَسَوَّى

خ	ف	أ	ر	أ	ف	ح	ع
ل	س	و	ح	د	س	ب	ح
ق	د	ر	و	و	م	أ	
ا	ل	أ	ع	ل	ى	ق	و
ح	س	ب	ق	أ	خ	ر	ج
ئ	ف	ى	ع	ر	م	ل	ا

Directions: Match the word
to its correct English meaning.

Meaning		Word
A. Brings forth		1- غُثَاءً
B. Created		2- الأَعْلَى
C. The pasture		3- خَلَقَ
D. Glorify	A	4- أَخْرَجَ
E. Who determined the creation		5- فَهَدَى
F. The Most High		6- سَبِّحِ
G. Dark or black		7- قَدَّرَ
H. Fashioned in due proportion		8- أَحْوَى
I. Then inspired them		9- فَسَوَّى
J. Withered Chaff		10- الْمَرْعَى

Picture Sequencing

Put the five illustrations below in order starting with verse number one. After you have ordered the illustrations write a few sentences about the meaning of each verse.

Section One Key

Verse number one worksheet (B)

II. God Almighty is the only one who controls our matters. This fact gives us a great sense of security in our lives. Always remember that Allah is the only one who gives us life and the only one who can take it away. We should treat others with mercy and justice as God always has the upper hand in this life and the hereafter. We should humble ourselves as we are all in a continues need of our creator and beloved Allah.

Verse number one worksheet (C)

1. The Most Holy: الْقُدُّوسُ
2. The Most perfect (free from any fault) : السَّلَام
3. The Maker : البَارِئُ
4. The Fashioner : المُصَوِّرُ
5. The All-provider : الرَّزَّاقُ

Verse number one worksheet (D)

I. سَبِّحِ آسْمَ رَبِّكَ ٱلْأَعْلَى

II. a. سَبِّحِ   b. ٱلْأَعْلَى   c. رَبِّكَ

Verse number two worksheet (B)

II. 1. a) God's Thrown   b) The pen   c) The Garden of Eden d) Our father Adam (PBUH)
2. "Be, and it is" كُن فَيَكُونُ
3. a) True.   b) False (Adam عليه السلام is the deputy of Allah on Earth)
   c) False (All creation has a well-defined purpose that is determined by Allah)
4. Allah taught Adam all the knowledge that he needs and he gave him the ability to learn.

Verse number two worksheet (D)

I. الذى خَلَقَ فَسَوّىٰ

II. 1. خَلَقَ   2. فَسَوّىٰ

Verse number three worksheet (B)

II. 1. a) Queen   b) Drones   c) worker honeybee
2. Allah سبحانه وتعالى
3. a) To be obedient to Allah and to perform their duties
   b) To be sincere and hard working as the honeybees are.
4. a) False
   b) False
   c) True
5. A drink of various colors in which there is healing for people.

The Most High

Section One Key

▬ Section one review worksheet (A)

ع	ح	ف	أ	ر	أ	ف	خ
ح	ب	س	د	ح	و	س	ل
أ	م	و	و	د	ر	د	ق
و	ق	ى	ل	ع	أ	ل	ا
ج	ر	خ	أ	ق	ب	س	ح
ا	ل	م	ر	ع	ى	ف	ئ

▬ Section one review worksheet (B)

1	2	3	4	5	6	7	8	9	10
J	F	B	A	I	D	E	G	H	C

▬ Section one review worksheet (C)

3

and Who determined [the creation] then inspired them .

2

Who created and fashioned in due proportion .

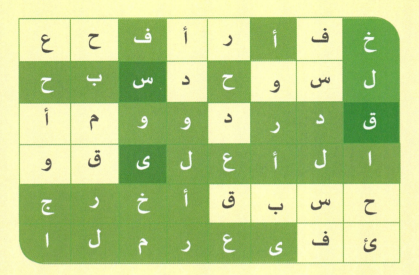

1

Glorify the name of your Lord, the Most High .

5

then makes it into withered chaff

4

and Who brings forth the pasture

Section Two
Verses 6-10 Worksheets

بِسْمِ اللَّهِ الرَّحْمَٰنِ الرَّحِيمِ

سَنُقْرِئُكَ فَلَا تَنسَىٰ (6) إِلَّا مَا شَاءَ اللَّهُ إِنَّهُ يَعْلَمُ
الْجَهْرَ وَمَا يَخْفَىٰ (7) وَنُيَسِّرُكَ لِلْيُسْرَىٰ (8) فَذَكِّرْ إِن
نَّفَعَتِ الذِّكْرَىٰ (9) سَيَذَّكَّرُ مَن يَخْشَىٰ (10)

We will teach you [the Qur'an], so you will not forget (6)
except what Allah wills, for indeed He knows what is
manifest and what is hidden (7) We will guide you to the
easy way (8) So remind, if the reminder should benefit (9)
He who fears Allah will take heed (10) ...

Color and Copy

فَلَا تَنسَىٰ

(So you will
not forget)

سَنُقْرِئُكَ

(We will teach
you the Quran)

------------------------------------1

------------------------------------1

------------------------------------2

------------------------------------2

------------------------------------3

------------------------------------3

------------------------------------4

------------------------------------4

------------------------------------5

------------------------------------5

------------------------------------6

------------------------------------6

I. Read the following short paragraph.

Prophet Muhammad (PBUH) is an illiterate man. He never read or wrote anything. He also was never a poet in spite the fact that poetry was very advanced among Arabs at the time the Quran was revealed. Prophet Muhammad (PBUH) recited the Quran which has a unique and perfect Arabic language that is free of error. The Arabic language of the Quran is similar to the language used by the Arabs, but at the same time it has different structures. The Quran has its own beauty and its words touch the hearts of all types of listeners. In spite of its beauty it is not considered to be poetry. A new style of Arabic literature was recited by Muhammad (PBUH). This was and still is a miracle since that no one could bring anything as unique as the language of the Quran!

Prophet Muhammad (PBUH) used to move his tongue in haste to memorize the Quran as soon as the Angel Gabriel read to him. He was concerned that he might forget because he couldn't read or write. Allah assured Muhammad (PBUH) that he will not forget and that he will teach him the meanings of the Quran.

You can read these meanings in the following verses:

Surat AL-Ala سُورَةُ الأَعْلَى	verse 6	سَنُقْرِئُكَ فَلَا تَنسَىٰ (6) We will teach you [the Qur'an], so you will not forget (6)
Surat AL-Qiyamah سُورَةُ القِيَامَه	(verse 16-17)	لَا تُحَرِّكْ بِهِ لِسَانَكَ لِتَعْجَلَ بِهِ (16) إِنَّ عَلَيْنَا جَمْعَهُ وَقُرْءَانَهُ (17) Do not move your tongue [O Prophet] in haste trying to memorize it (16) It is upon Us to make you memorize and recite it (17)
Surat Ta-ha سُورَة طَه	erse 114)	فَتَعَالَى ٱللَّهُ ٱلْمَلِكُ ٱلْحَقُّ وَلَا تَعْجَلْ بِٱلْقُرْءَانِ مِن قَبْلِ أَن يُقْضَىٰ إِلَيْكَ وَحْيُهُ وَقُل رَّبِّ زِدْنِي عِلْمًا (114) So Exalted is Allah, the True Sovereign. Do not hasten to [recite] the Qur'an before its revelation to you is concluded, and say, "My Lord, increase me in knowledge." (114)

II. Answer the following questions:

1. Why was prophet Muhammad (PBUH) concerned when he recited the Holy Quran after the Angel Gabriel read to him? ···
   ··

2. What did Allah order prophet Muhammad (PBUH) not to do? ·····················

3. According to the verses above who is in charge of preserving the Holy Quran?
   ··

4. True or false:

a) Prophet Muhammad (PBUH) is a good poet.

b) The Arabic language of the Quran is unique and has a new style.

c) Some famous Arabic poets were able to bring literature that is equal to the literature of the Quran.

d) Angel Gabriel is the Angel responsible for recording people's deeds.

5. What is the supplication (دُعَاء) that we learn from Surat Ta-ha (verse 114) above?

··

I. Color and Copy

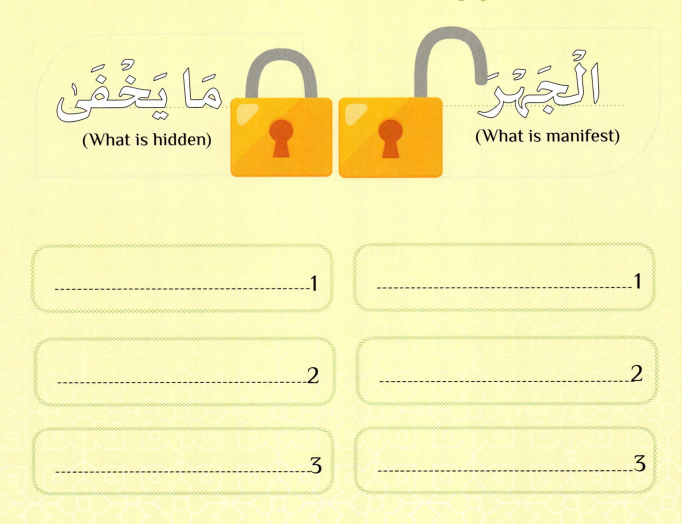

مَا يَخْفَىٰ
(What is hidden)

الْجَهْرَ
(What is manifest)

-----------------------------1

-----------------------------1

-----------------------------2

-----------------------------2

-----------------------------3

-----------------------------3

II. Copy the complete verse below

إِلَّا مَا شَاءَ اللَّهُ إِنَّهُ يَعْلَمُ الْجَهْرَ وَمَا يَخْفَىٰ

except what Allah wills, for indeed He knows
what is manifest and what is hidden

.... 1

.... 2

.... 3

The Most High

I. Copy

وَنُيَسِّرُكَ لِلْيُسْرَىٰ

(We will Guide you to the easy way)

....1

....2

....3

II. Answer the following question

According to verse 8 what is the easiest way to paradise?

....

....

....

....

....

There are many examples of good deeds that a person can sincerely perform to please Allah.
Reflect on verse 8 below by listing some good deeds that you personally can easily perform to please Allah.

I. Color and Copy

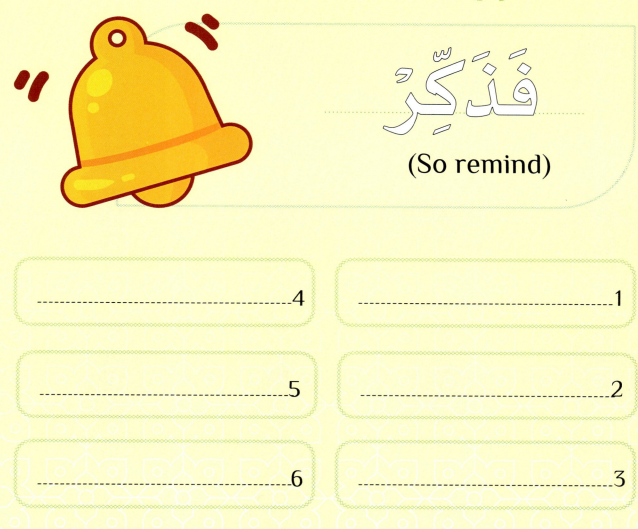

فَذَكِّرْ

(So remind)

4 ....

1 ....

5 ....

2 ....

6 ....

3 ....

II. Copy the complete verse below

فَذَكِّرْ إِن نَّفَعَتِ الذِّكْرَى

So remind, if the reminder should benefit

1 ....

2 ....

3 ....

The Most High

31

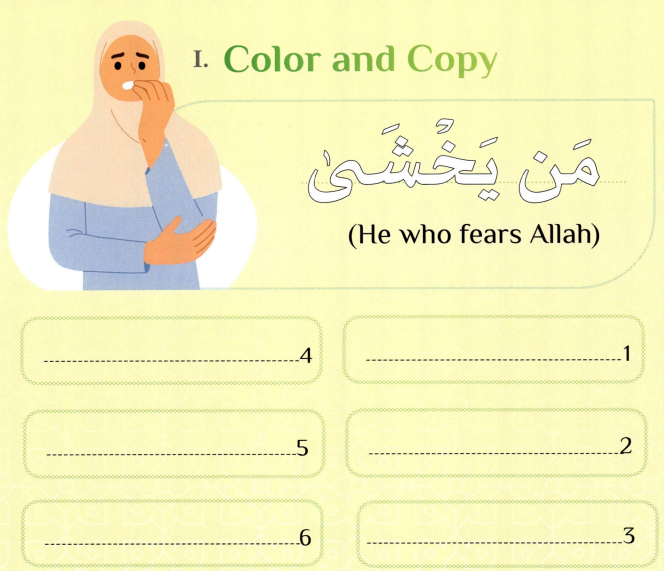

I. Color and Copy

مَن يَخْشَىٰ

(He who fears Allah)

----------------------------------4   ----------------------------------1

----------------------------------5   ----------------------------------2

----------------------------------6   ----------------------------------3

II. Unscramble the following words from verse ten and then copy the complete verse below.

يَخْشَىٰ / مَن / سَيَذَّكَّرُ

He who fears Allah will take heed

....1

....2

....3

I. Read the following short paragraph.

There are six pillars of faith in Islam. Prophet Muhammad (PBUH) clearly stated in his Hadith that:" Faith means to believe in Allah, His angels, His books, His Messengers, the Last Day, and the Divine Decree, both good and bad.

قَالَ رَسُولُ الله صَلَى اللهُ عَلَيه وسَلَمَ عندَمَا سَألهُ جبريل عليه السَّلام عَن الإيمَان:

{أَن تُؤْمِنَ بِاللهِ وَمَلائِكَتِه وَكُتُبِه ورُسُلِه وَاليَوم الآخِر، وَتُؤْمِنَ بِالقَدَرِ خَيْرِه وَشَرِهِ}

Muslims believe that the Last Day is the day when all humans are going to be "resurrected" from the dead. On this day all people are going to be called to account. All of our good deeds are counted in our favor on this Last day (also called Judgment Day). At the same time, all of our bad deeds are held against us on Judgement Day.

People of faith and reflection believe in their hearts that Allah will hold them responsible for all of their deeds. They also believe that His ultimate justice is the truth. Thus, people of faith and reflection are motivated to refrain from doing bad deeds. The more aware they are about Allah's Might and ability over them the more fearful they are about committing bad deeds. This fear of committing bad deeds when Allah is in observation (بِالمِرْصَاد) is what verse ten is referring to. We can also see a similar meaning in Surat An-Nazi at (سُورَةُ النَّازِعَات) verses 40 and 41 below:

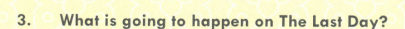

وَأَمَّا مَنْ خَافَ مَقَامَ رَبِّهِ ـ وَنَهَى آلنَّفْسَ عَنِ آلْهَوَى (40) فَإِنَّ آلْجَنَّةَ هِيَ آلْمَأْوَى (41)

But those who feared standing before their Lord and restrained themselves from evil desires (40)
Paradise will surely be their abode (41)

II. Answer the following questions:

1. **What are the six pillars of faith in Islam?**

A)	D)
B)	E)
C)	F)

2. **What is another name for The Last Day?**

   ....

3. **What is going to happen on The Last Day?**

   ....

4. **Who is always in observation (بِالمِرْصَاد)?** ....

5. **How could a believer increase their fear of Allah?**

   ....

   ....

6. **Who is recording our good and bad deeds in our record (صَحِيفَةُ أَعْمَالِنَا)?**

   ....

7. **True or False:**

   a) Only bad people have evil desires.

   b) The word abode means: a place of residence; a house or home.

   c) Allah is forgiving and deeds are not important as long as we believe.

   d) People of faith and reflection are fearful of Allah because they believe that they are accountable for ALL of their actions in this life.

   e) It is a bad quality to be fearful of Allah.

Word Search!
Quran Chapter 87

Find each of the words in the box below.
Words may go across, down, up, or diagonally.

يَخْشَى   الْجَهْرَ   سَنُقْرِئُكَ

لِلْيُسْرَى   نُيَسِّرُكَ   فَذَكِّر

يَخْفَى   لاَ تَنْسَى

ص	ل	ا	ل	ج	ه	ر	ي
ث	ا	س	ل	ف	ر	ذ	خ
ف	ت	ء	ي	خ	ش	ى	ف
ح	ن	ي	س	ر	ك	ه	ى
ت	س	ف	ر	ف	ذ	ك	ر
ع	ى	ن	ى	ه	خ	ت
ر	ق	ك	ء	ر	ق	ن	س

Directions: Match the word
to its correct English meaning.

Meaning	Word

Meaning		Word
A. So remind		1- يَخْشَى
B. What is Manifest		2- فَلَا تَنسَى
C. So you will not forget		3- الْجَهْرَ
D. What is Hidden	A	4- مُذَكِّرٌ
E. The easy way of Islam		5- يَخْفَى
F. We will guide you		6- سَنُقْرِئُكَ
G. He who Fears Allah		7- نُيَسِّرُكَ
H. We will teach you the Quran		8- لِلْيُسْرَى

Picture Sequencing

Put the five illustrations below in order starting with verse number six. After you have ordered the illustrations color each word.

فَذَكِّرْ ⬜   يَخْفَىٰ ⬜

الْجَهْرَ ⬜ الْيُسْرَىٰ ⬜

سَنُقْرِئُكَ ⬜

Section Two Key

Verse number (6) worksheet (B)

1. He was concerned that he might forget the Quran since that he can't read or write.

2. Allah ordered Muhammad (PBUH) not to move his tongue in haste to memorize the Quran.

3. Allah All Mighty is in charge of preserving the Quran forever.

4. a) False - Prophet Muhammad (PBUH)is NOT a poet.
   b) True
   c) False - No one was or is capable of bringing anything such as the Quran.
   d) False - Angel Gabriel is the Angel that is sent to all the prophets with the word of God.

5. وَقُل رَّبِّ زِدْنِي عِلْمَاً   (My Lord, increase me in knowledge)

Verse number (8) worksheet (A)

II. Islam and it's way of life. Islam teaches us about monotheism and the things to perform in order to please Allah. It also teaches us about the things to avoid in order to live a happy, peaceful and productive life.

Verse number (10) worksheet (A)

II. سَيَذَّكَّرُ مَن يَخْشَىٰ

Taking heed means to give serious attention to Allah's warnings, commands, and advice and to be careful about them.

Verse number (10) worksheet (B)

1. The six pillers of faith are to believe in:
   a) Allah
   b) His angels
   c) His books
   d) His Messengers
   e) The Last Day
   f) The Devine Decree (both good and bad)

2. Day of Judgment

3. All people are going to be called to account.

4. Allah   سُبْحَانَهُ وَتَعَالَى

5. a) By always being aware of Allah's Might and ability over them and by increasing their Knowledge of Allah سُبْحَانَهُ وَتَعَالَى and his attributes.
   b) By always being aware that Allah is in observation of all of his creation
   (بِالْمِرْصَاد).

Section Two Key

6. There are two angels assigned for this purpose. One angel is on our right side recording our good deeds and one angel is on our left side recording our bad deeds.

7. a) False (All humans have desires that could be good or bad and should be aware of temptations and the Devil's whisper)

   b) True

   c) False (it true that Allah is forgiving, but at the same time we are going to be called to account for all of our deeds)

   d) True

   e) False (it is a good and beneficial quality to be fearful of Allah since that this feeling will prevent us from committing harm against ourselves, others, and all of the other creation including animals, plants, etc.)

▬ Section (2) review worksheet (A)

ي	ر	ه	ج	ل	ا	ل	ص
خ	ذ	ر	ف	ل	س	ا	ث
ف	ى	ش	خ	ي	ت	ء	ف
ى	ه	ك	ر	س	ي	ن	ح
ر	ك	ذ	ف	ر	ف	س	ت
ت	خ	ه	ن	ى	ء	ى	ع
س	ن	ق	ر	ء	ك	ق	ر

▬ Section (2) review worksheet (B)

1	2	3	4	5	6	7	8
G	C	B	A	D	H	F	E

▬ Section (2) review worksheet (C)

5 فَذَكِّرْ   4 الْيُسْرَىٰ   3 يَخْفَىٰ   2 الْجَهْرَ   1 سَنُقْرِئُكَ

بِسْمِ ٱللَّهِ ٱلرَّحْمَٰنِ ٱلرَّحِيمِ

وَيَتَجَنَّبُهَا ٱلْأَشْقَى (11) ٱلَّذِي يَصْلَى ٱلنَّارَ ٱلْكُبْرَى (12) ثُمَّ لَا يَمُوتُ فِيهَا وَلَا يَحْيَى (13) قَدْ أَفْلَحَ مَن تَزَكَّى (14) وَذَكَرَ ٱسْمَ رَبِّهِ فَصَلَّى (15)

but the wretched will avoid it (11) who will enter the
Great Fire (12) wherein he will neither die nor live (13)
Indeed, he who purifies himself will attain success (14)
and remembers his Lord's Name and prays (15) ...

I. Copy the word

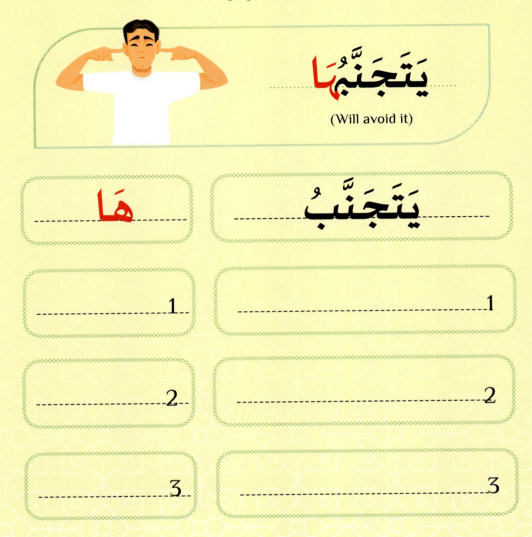

يَتَجَنَّبُهَا

(Will avoid it)

هَا

يَتَجَنَّبُ

_____ 1

_____ 1

_____ 2

_____ 2

_____ 3

_____ 3

II. a) Why are the last two letters red in color?
b) What does the (هَا) indicate ?

_____

_____

_____

_____

I. Color and Copy

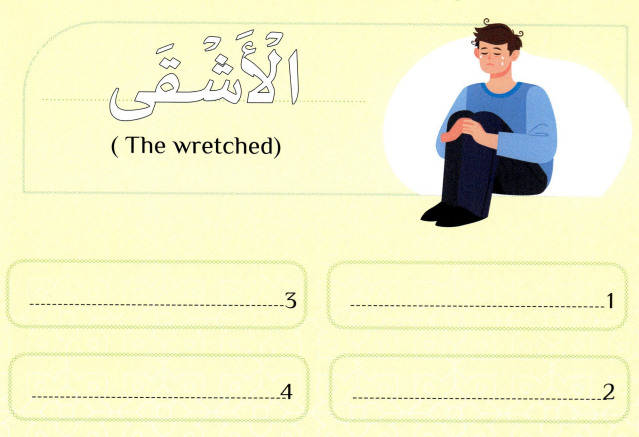

الْأَشْقَى

(The wretched)

```
---------------------3        ---------------------1
```

```
---------------------4        ---------------------2
```

II. Copy the complete verse below

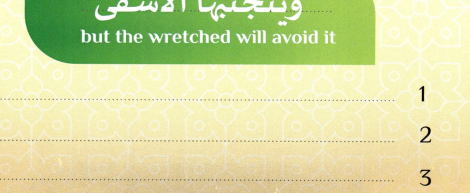

وَيَتَجَنَّبُهَا الْأَشْقَى
but the wretched will avoid it

```
....................................................... 1
```

```
....................................................... 2
```

```
....................................................... 3
```

Match the arabic word from the box below to its correct English translation, then copy it in the appropirate box

	English translation	Word in Arabic
	Avoid	-------------------- -1
	Wretched	-------------------- -2
	The reminder	-------------------- -3

الذِّكْرَى   الْأَشْقَى   يَتَجَنَّبُ

Color and Copy

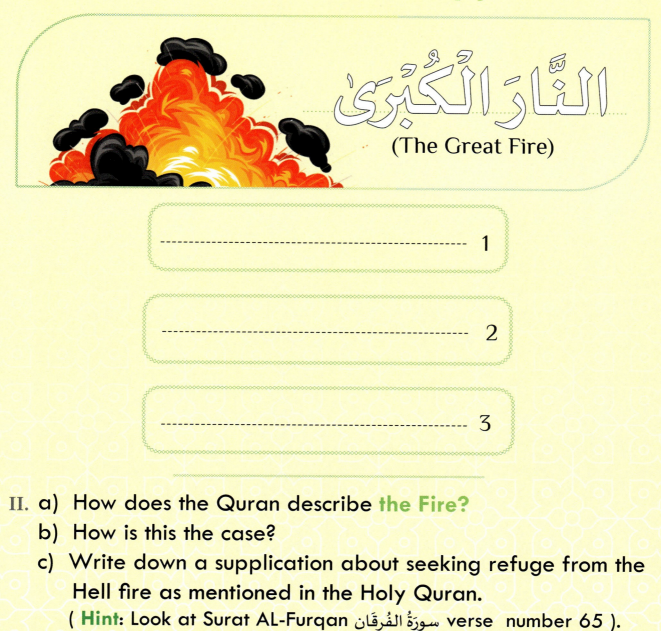

النَّارُ الْكُبْرَى

(The Great Fire)

--- 1

--- 2

--- 3

II. a) How does the Quran describe the Fire?

b) How is this the case?

c) Write down a supplication about seeking refuge from the
Hell fire as mentioned in the Holy Quran.
(Hint: Look at Surat AL-Furqan سورَةُ الفُرقَان verse number 65).

....
....
....
....
....
....

I. Unscramble the following words from verse 12
and then **copy** the complete verse
five times on the lines provided below.

النَّارَ / يَصْلَى / الَّذِي / الْكُبْرَى

who will enter the Great Fire

....1

....2

....3

....4

....5

II. **a)** Which vocabulary word above means (**Great**) ?

....

b) Which vocabulary word above means (**Fire**) ?

....

c) Which vocabulary word above means (**Who**) ?

....

Color and Copy

(Nor live) لَايَحْيَى

(Neither die) لَايَمُوتُ

--------------------------------1

--------------------------------1

--------------------------------2

--------------------------------2

--------------------------------3

--------------------------------3

II. **Read** Quran chapter 4 (سورة النساء) verse 56 meaning.
Reflect on how this relates to the explanation of
neither die nor live

....

....

....

The Most High

I. **Unscramble** the following words from verse 13 and then **copy** the complete verse five times on the lines provided below.

لَا يَمُوتُ / وَلَا يَحْيَى / فِيهَا / ثُمَّ

wherein he will neither die nor live

.... 1

.... 2

.... 3

.... 4

.... 5

II. a) **Which vocabulary word above means (Neither die) ?**

....

b) Which vocabulary word above means (Nor live) ?

....

c) Where does this take place ?

....

Color and Copy

أَفْلَحَ

(Attain success)

-------------------------------------3

-------------------------------------1

-------------------------------------4

-------------------------------------2

II. **Draw or Describe** an example of something that you successfully achieved today to please Allah.

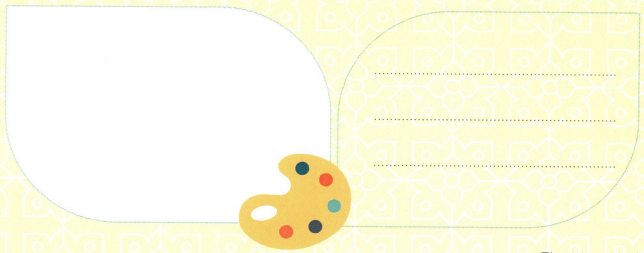

Color and Copy

تَزَكَّىٰ

(Purifies him/her self)

---

3 ----------------------------------

1 ----------------------------------

4 ----------------------------------

2 ----------------------------------

II. How could someone purify him/herself?
(**Hint:** the answer is given in the next verse # 15)
Write or illustrate your answer below.

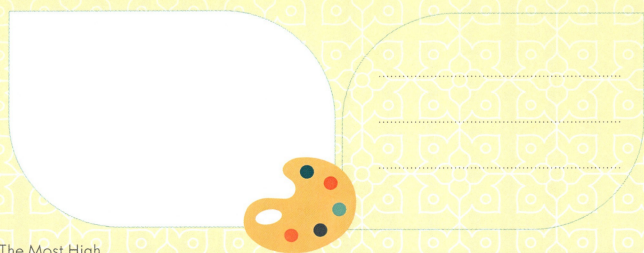

....

....

....

Copy the following words from verse 14
three times each below.

قَدْ

------------------3   ------------------2   ------------------1

أَفْلَحَ

------------------3   ------------------2   ------------------1

مَن

------------------3   ------------------2   ------------------1

تَزَكَّى

------------------3   ------------------2   ------------------1

Color and Copy

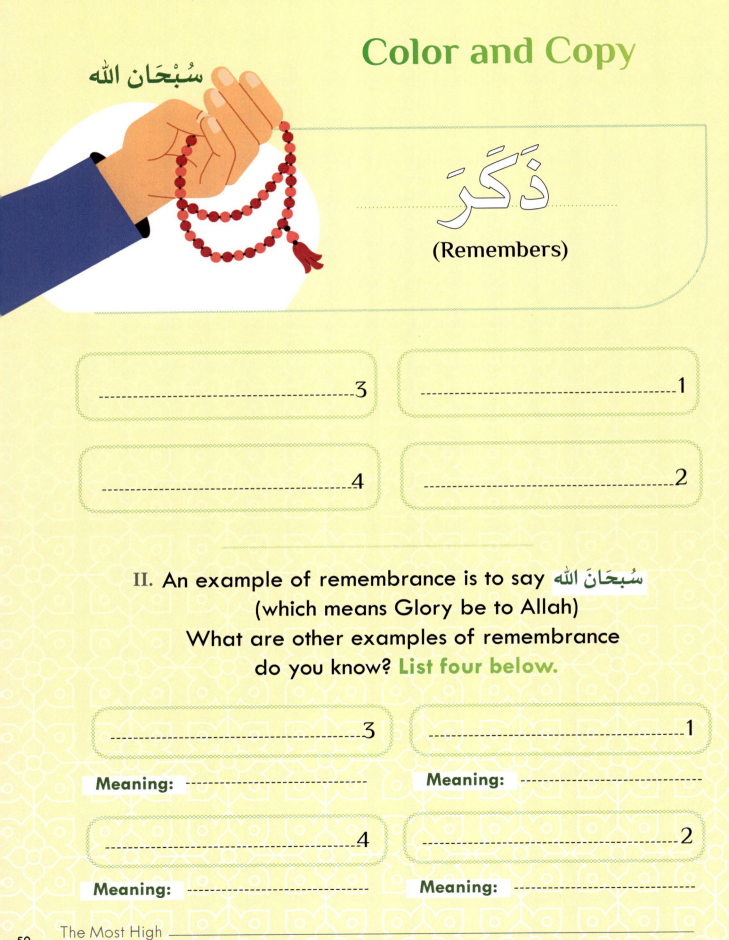

سُبْحَان الله

ذَكَرَ

(Remembers)

_____ 3   _____ 1

_____ 4   _____ 2

II. An example of remembrance is to say سُبْحَانَ الله
(which means Glory be to Allah)
What are other examples of remembrance
do you know? **List four below.**

_____ 3   _____ 1

Meaning: _____   **Meaning:** _____

_____ 4   _____ 2

Meaning: _____   **Meaning:** _____

Color and Copy

فَصَلَّىٰ

(Prays)

--------------------------------3

--------------------------------4

II. Answer the following questions:

1. How many times a day do Muslims pray?
----

2. What is Athan? --------------------------------------

3. How should Muslims prepare for prayers? ------------------------
----

4. What direction or place do Muslims face when they perform their daily prayers? (Where is Qibla located?)
----

5. How is Friday prayer different? ------------------------------
----

Circle the correct meaning of each word from verse 15

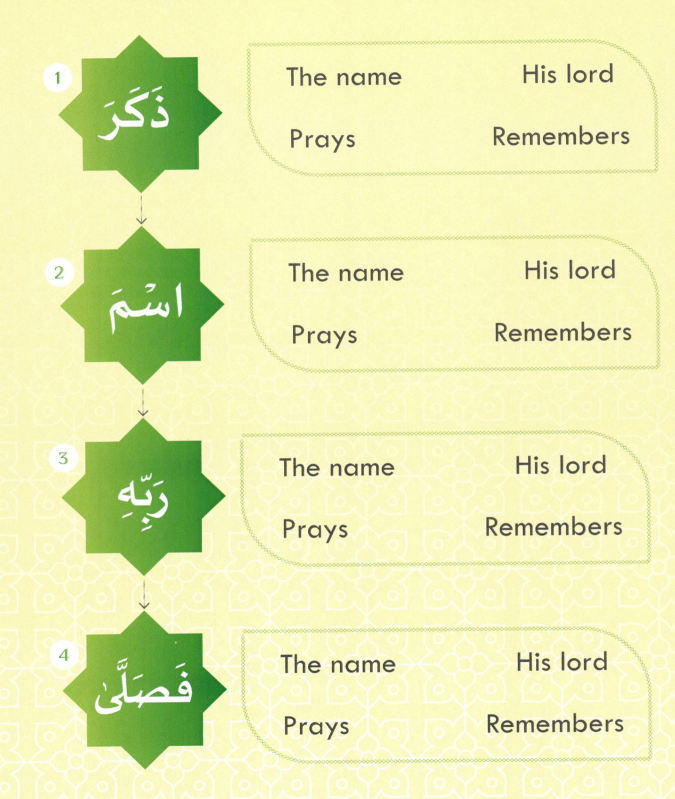

1 ذَكَرَ

The name   His lord

Prays   Remembers

2 اسْمَ

The name   His lord

Prays   Remembers

3 رَبِّهِ

The name   His lord

Prays   Remembers

4 فَصَلَّى

The name   His lord

Prays   Remembers

I. **Read the following paragraph & then answer the questions.**

Allah All Mighty tells us that we prefer the temporary life of this world as opposed to our eternal life in the hereafter. Scholars recommend a state by which this world's pleasures and materialistic things are in our hands rather than in our hearts. Which means that our hearts are in a constant state of remembrance and awareness of Allah and the hereafter.

Questions:

1. Is it okay to love something of this world?

   ....

   ....

   ....

   ....

2. What happens when you lose something that is very dear to your heart?

   ....

   ....

   ....

   ....

Word Search!
Quran Chapter 87

Find each of the words in the box below.
Words may go across, down, up, or diagonally.

أَفْلَحَ		تَزَكَّى		لَا يَمُوتُ
الْكُبْرَى		الْأَشْقَى		فَصَلَّى
يَتَجَنَّبُهَا		النَّارَ		

ي	ى	ق	ش	أ	ل	ا
ت	أ	ف	ل	ح	ك	ل
ج	ر	ا	ن	ل	ا	ك
ن	ى	ج	ص	ي	ه	ب
ب	ك	ش	م	و	م	ر
ه	ز	و	ر	أ	ت	ى
ا	ت	ى	ل	ص	ف	ق

The Most High _____

Directions: Match the word to its correct English meaning.

Meaning	Word

Meaning

A. Prays

B. The wretched

C. Will avoid it

D. The Great

E. Purifies self

F. Attain success

G. Nor live

H. His/her lord

Word

1- أَفْلَحَ [ ]

2- الْكُبْرَى [ ]

3- تَزَكَّىٰ [ ]

4- فَصَلَّىٰ [A]

5- لَا يَحْيَىٰ [ ]

6- الْأَشْقَى [ ]

7- يَتَجَنَّبُهَا [ ]

8- رَبِّهِ [ ]

Complete writing the verses below

11 وَيَتَجَنَّبُهَا

....

12 الَّذِى ....

....

....

13 ثُمَّ لَا ....

....

....

14 قَدْ ....

....

15 وَذَكَرَ ....

....

Section Three Key

Verse number (11) worksheet (A)

II. a) The last two letters are red in color because they are NOT part of the verb (يَتَجَنَّبُ).
This verb means: will avoid.

b) It indicates a word from verse 9. This word is (الذِّكْرَى) which means: the reminder.
The (هَا) is equivalent to "it" in the English language.

Verse number (11) worksheet (C)

1. يَتَجَنَّبُ
2. الأَشْقَى
3. الذِّكْرَى

Verse number (12) worksheet (A)

II. a) The great Fire or the greatest fire.

b) A description indicating the extreme heat and pain.

c) وَالَّذِينَ يَقُولُونَ رَبَّنَا اصْرِفْ عَنَّا عَذَابَ جَهَنَّمَ إِنَّ عَذَابَهَا كَانَ غَرَامًا

And those who say:" Our Lord, turn the punishment of Hell away from us, for its punishment is unrelenting (its punishment is ever adhering)

Verse number (12) worksheet (B)

I. الَّذِي يَصْلَى النَّارَ الْكُبْرَى

II. a) الْكُبْرَى

b) النَّارَ

Verse number (13) worksheet (A)

II.

إِنَّ الَّذِينَ كَفَرُوا بِآيَاتِنَا سَوْفَ نُصْلِيهِمْ نَارًا كُلَّمَا نَضِجَتْ جُلُودُهُمْ بَدَّلْنَاهُمْ جُلُودًا غَيْرَهَا لِيَذُوقُوا الْعَذَابَ إِنَّ اللَّهَ كَانَ عَزِيزًا حَكِيمًا

Those who reject Our verses, We will cast them into the Fire. Whenever their skins are burnt through, We will replace them with fresh skins, so that they may taste the punishment. Indeed, Allah is All-Mighty, All-Wise.

Verse number (13) worksheet (B)

I. ثُمَّ لَا يَمُوتُ فِيهَا وَلَا يَحْيَى

II. a) لَا يَحْيَى   b) لَا يَمُوتُ   c) The Great Fire النَّارَ الْكُبْرَى

Verse number (15) worksheet (A)

II. 1. لا إلهَ إلا الله (There is no God but Allah)

2. أَسْتَغْفِرُ الله (I ask Allah for forgiveness)

3. اللهُ أَكْبَر (Allah is the greatest)

4. الحَمْدُ لله (Praise be to Allah)

Section Three Key

Verse number (15) worksheet (B)

1. Muslims pray five times a day
2. Athan (الأذان للصلاة) is the call for prayer. It is made five times a day to indicate the start of the time for each prayer.
3. By performing ablution (وُضُوء)
4. Qibla is towards the Kaaba (الكَعْبَه) in the city of Makkah مكة المكرمة
5. It only has two Rakaas ركعتان and this makes it shorter than the usual midday prayer (صلاة الظهر). It is also preceded with a sermon (خُطْبَه) by the Imam.

Verse number (15) worksheet (C)

1. Remembers
2. The name
3. His lord
4. Prays

Verse number (15) worksheet (D)

1. It is perfectly okay to love the Halal and good things that Allah سبحانه وتعالى has given us. However, we have to keep our priorities in perspective and always love Allah and his Prophet the most.

2. We know that everything happens by Allah's wish and knowledge. We accept what Allah mandates for us (good and bad). We always seek refuge and comfort performing remembrance and prayers as prescribed in verse number 15 of this Surah الأعلى.

Section (3) review worksheet (A)

ا	ل	أ	ش	ق	ى	ي
ل	ك	ح	ل	ف	أ	ت
ك	ا	ل	ن	ا	ر	ج
ب	ه	ي	ص	ج	ى	ن
ر	م	و	م	ش	ك	ب
ى	ت	أ	ر	و	ز	ه
ق	ف	ص	ل	ى	ت	ا

Section (3) review worksheet (B)

1	2	3	4
F	D	E	A
5	6	7	8
G	B	C	H

Section (3) review worksheet (C)

وَيَتَجَنَّبُهَا ٱلْأَشْقَى (11) ٱلَّذِي يَصْلَى ٱلنَّارَ ٱلْكُبْرَى (12) قَدْ أَفْلَحَ مَن تَزَكَّىٰ (14)
ثُمَّ لَا يَمُوتُ فِيهَا وَلَا يَحْيَىٰ (13) وَذَكَرَ ٱسْمَ رَبِّهِ ۦ فَصَلَّىٰ (15)

بِسْمِ اللَّهِ الرَّحْمَٰنِ الرَّحِيمِ

بَل تُؤْثِرُونَ ٱلْحَيَوٰةَ ٱلدُّنْيَا (16) وَٱلْأَخِرَةُ خَيْرٌ
وَأَبْقَىٰ (17) إِنَّ هَٰذَا لَفِي ٱلصُّحُفِ ٱلْأُولَىٰ (18)
صُحُفِ إِبْرَٰهِيمَ وَمُوسَىٰ (19)

But you prefer the life of this world (16) even though the Hereafter is better and more lasting (17) Indeed, this was in the earlier Scriptures (18) the Scriptures of Abraham and Moses (19)

Read the words and
then copy them below

الْحَيَوٰةَ الدُّنْيَا

(The life of this world)

بَلْ تُؤْثِرُونَ

(But you prefer)

--1

--1

--2

--2

--3

--3

--4

--4

I. Read the following Hadith and passage....

Narrated Abu Huraira:

Prophet Muhammad (PBUH) said:

" Let the slave of Dinar (Gold coin) and Dirham (Silver coin), of Quantify and Khamisa (black-boarded cloak) perish; as he is pleased if these things are given to him, and if not, he is displeased..........

عن النبي (صلى الله عليه وسلم) قال: تَعِسَ عَبْدُ الدينار وَعَبْدُ الدِرْهَم وَعَبْدُ الخميصة، إن أُعْطِي رَضِي، وَإِن لَمْ يُعْطَ سَخِطَ، تَعِسَ وانتَكَس.........................)

In this Hadith Prophet Muhammad (PBUH) is warning us about a life of shallow pleasures and materialism. He is warning us about a life that is lacking in ethical and spiritual matters. Prophet Muhammad describes a type of people who are happy only when possession such as gold coins, silver coins, and fancy garments are given to them. When Allah gives this type of people these things, they are satisfied with him and when Allah doesn't give them these things, they are displeased and angry with him.

The teachings of Islam direct us to earn a good living for ourselves and our families and communities in lawful and ethical ways. It teaches us to be charitable and spiritual at the same time. Furthermore, we have to be pleased with what Allah has given us and satisfied with his decree (the good and the bad). In Islam competition is encouraged in all aspects of life as long as it is Halal حَلال (permissible by clear Islamic Laws). Halal earnings and goodness is encouraged as long as we have a balanced and spiritual lives. Working all the time in order to earn all types of possessions and missing out on our daily religious obligations such as prayers is discouraged in Islam. This unbalanced way of life will only lead to great loss in this life and more importantly, in the hereafter.

II. Answer the following questions:

1. What is Prophet Muhammad (PBUH) is warning us about?

   ....

   ....

2. What does the Arabic word Dinar دِينَار mean?

3. What does the Arabic word Dirham دِرْهَم mean?

   ....

4. What does the Arabic word Khamisa خَمِيصَه mean?

   ....

5. True or False:
   a) Competition is discouraged according to Islam teachings.
   b) Muslims are discouraged from looking sharp and clean since that they are preoccupied with acts of worship.
   c) It is not sinful to love gold and silver as long as it is earned through Halal ways and Zakat is given.
   d) One should be angry when Allah gives them a family of humble possessions.

Color and then cop

خَيْرٌ وَأَبْقَى

(Better and more lasting)

الْأَخِرَةُ

(The Hereafter)

_____1

_____2

_____3

_____4

_____5

_____1

_____2

_____3

_____4

_____5

Answer the question below

by writing the meanings from each Quran chapter and verses listed below.

1

سورة الغاشية
Quran Chapter 88, Verse 10-16

....
....
....
....
....
....
....

2

سورة الإنسان
Quran Chapter 76, Verse 12-21

....
....
....
....
....
....
....
....

Question:
Why is the hereafter better for a believer?

3

سورة يس
Quran Chapter 36, Verse 55-58

....
....
....
....
....
....

4

سورة الواقعه
Quran Chapter 56, Verse 25-26

....
....
....
....
....
....

Look at the diagrams below.

1. Which case is God warning us about: one, two, or three?

2. How do you know?

1

....
....
....
....
....

الْحَيَوٰةَ الدُّنْيَا
(Life of this world)

الْأَخِرَةُ
(Hereafter)

2

....
....
....
....
....
....

الْحَيَوٰةَ الدُّنْيَا
(Life of this world)

الْأَخِرَةُ
(Hereafter)

3

....
....
....
....
....
....

الْأَخِرَةُ
(Hereafter)

الْحَيَوٰةَ الدُّنْيَا
(Life of this world)

I. **Color and Copy**

الْأُوْلَى

(Earlier)

الصُّحُفِ

(Scriptures)

------------1	------------1
------------2	------------2

II. **Unscramble** the following words from verse 18 and then **copy** the complete verse four times below.

الْأُوْلَى / الصُّحُفِ / إِنَّ / لَفِي / هَٰذَا

In deed this was in the earlier Scriptures

------------1

------------2

------------3

------------4

Copy the words below

صُحُفِ

the Scriptures

----------5	----------3	----------1
----------6	----------4	----------2

وَمُوسَىٰ

Musa

إِبْرَٰهِيمَ

lbrahim

----------1	----------1
----------2	----------2
----------3	----------3
----------4	----------4
----------5	----------5
----------6	----------6

Answer the following questions.

1. What is the name of the first prophet?

----

2. What is the name of the last prophet?

----

3. What are the names of the two prophets mentioned in this chapter of the Holy Quran?

----

4. Reflect on the lessons learned from Ibrahim and Musa scriptures as repeated here in this chapter of the Quran...

The Most High

Word Search!
Quran Chapter 87

Find each of the words in the box below.
Words may go across, down, up, or diagonally.

أَبْقَىٰ	الصُّحُفِ
الْأُولَىٰ	مُوسَىٰ	خَيْرٌ
الْأَخِرَةُ	الدُّنْيَا	تُؤْثِرُونَ

ا	ل	ص	ح	ف	خ	ا	ق
خ	ث	ا	ل	أ	و	ل	ى
ت	ؤ	ث	ر	ن	د	ى
ه	ر	خ	أ	ل	ا	ن	س
ن	أ	ب	ى	ق	ر	ي	و
خ	ي	ر	م	ص	ب	ا	م

Directions: Match the word
to its correct English meaning.

Meaning	Word

Meaning		Word
A. Ibrahim		1- الْأَخِرَةُ
B. Prefer		2- مُوسَىٰ
C. This world life		3- الصُّحُفِ
D. Hereafter	C	4- الْحَيَوٰةَ الدُّنْيَا
E. More Lasting		5- أَبْقَىٰ
F. The earlier		6- تُؤْثِرُونَ
G. Musa		7- إِبْرَٰهِيمَ
H. The scriptures		8- الْأُولَىٰ

Complete writing the verses below

16 بَلْ ....

17 .... وَالْآخِرَةُ ....

18 إِنَّ هَـٰذَا ....

19 صُحُفِ ....

Section Four Key

Verse number (16) worksheet (B)

II. 1. Prophet Muhammad (PBUH) is warning us about a life of shallow pleasures and materialism. He is warning us about a life that is lacking in ethical and spiritual matters.

2. Gold coin

3. Silver coin

4. Black boarded cloak

5. True or False:

a) False: Competition is encouraged according to Islamic teachings as long as it is done Halal way and produces Halal حلال (permissible by clear Islamic Laws).

b) False: Muslims are encouraged to look sharp and clean since that they strive to be well rounded and balanced people that also make time for acts of worship.

c) True.

d) False: One should be grateful for what Allah has given them, but at the same time ask Allah and have an action plan to change their circumstances to better ones. A Muslim is also encouraged (if he/she can) to help others change their circumstances to better ones.

Verse number (17) worksheet (B)

1- في جَنَّةٍ عَالِيَةٍ (10) لَا تَسْمَعُ فِيهَا لَاغِيَةً (11) فِيهَا عَيْنٌ جَارِيَةٌ (12) فِيهَا سُرُرٌ مَرْفُوعَةٌ (13) وَأَكْوَابٌ مَوْضُوعَةٌ (14) وَنَمَارِقُ مَصْفُوفَةٌ (15) وَزَرَابِيُّ مَبْثُوثَةٌ (16)

in an elevated garden (10) wherein no idle talk will be heard (11) There will be a flowing spring (12) and couches raised high (13) and cups placed ready (14) and cushions lined up (15) and splendid carpets spread out (16)

2- وَجَزَاهُم بِمَا صَبَرُوا جَنَّةً وَحَرِيرًا (12) مُّتَّكِئِينَ فِيهَا عَلَى الْأَرَائِكِ لَا يَرَوْنَ فِيهَا شَمْسًا وَلَا زَمْهَرِيرًا (13) وَدَانِيَةً عَلَيْهِمْ ظِلَالُهَا وَذُلِّلَتْ قُطُوفُهَا تَذْلِيلًا (14) وَيُطَافُ عَلَيْهِم بِآنِيَةٍ مِن فِضَّةٍ وَأَكْوَابٍ كَانَتْ قَوَارِيرَا (15) قَوَارِيرَ مِن فِضَّةٍ قَدَّرُوهَا تَقْدِيرًا (16) وَيُسْقَوْنَ فِيهَا كَأْسًا كَانَ مِزَاجُهَا زَنجَبِيلًا (17) عَيْنًا فِيهَا تُسَمَّىٰ سَلْسَبِيلًا (18) ۞ وَيَطُوفُ عَلَيْهِمْ وِلْدَانٌ مُّخَلَّدُونَ إِذَا رَأَيْتَهُمْ حَسِبْتَهُمْ لُؤْلُؤًا مَّنثُورًا (19) وَإِذَا رَأَيْتَ ثَمَّ رَأَيْتَ نَعِيمًا وَمُلْكًا كَبِيرًا (20) عَلَيْهِمْ ثِيَابُ سُندُسٍ خُضْرٌ وَإِسْتَبْرَقٌ وَحُلُّوا أَسَاوِرَ مِن فِضَّةٍ وَسَقَاهُمْ رَبُّهُمْ شَرَابًا طَهُورًا (21)

and will reward them for their perseverance with Paradise and garments of silk (12) They will recline therein on adorned couches; neither feeling scorching heat nor freezing cold (13) with shady branches spread above them, and clusters of fruit will be made within their reach (14) They will be served frequently with silver vessels and crystal cups (15) crystalline goblets of silver, filled precisely as desired (16) They will be given a glass [of wine] flavored with ginger (17) from a spring therein called Salsabil (18) They will be served by eternal young boys; if you see them, you would think that they are scattered pearls (19) If you were to look around, you would see bliss and a vast dominion (20) They will be dressed in garments of fine green silk and rich brocade, and will be adorned with bracelets of silver, and their Lord will give them a pure drink (21)

3- إِنَّ أَصْحَابَ الْجَنَّةِ الْيَوْمَ فِي شُغُلٍ فَاكِهُونَ (55) هُمْ وَأَزْوَاجُهُمْ فِي ظِلَالٍ عَلَى الْأَرَائِكِ مُتَّكِئُونَ (56) لَهُمْ فِيهَا فَاكِهَةٌ وَلَهُم مَّا يَدَّعُونَ (57) سَلَامٌ قَوْلًا مِن رَّبٍّ رَّحِيمٍ (58)

Indeed, on that Day the people of Paradise will be busy enjoying themselves (55) they and their spouses will be reclining on couches in the shade (56) They will have therein fruits and all what they ask for (57) "Peace": a word from a Most Merciful Lord (58)

4- لَا يَسْمَعُونَ فِيهَا لَغْوًا وَلَا تَأْثِيمًا (25) إِلَّا قِيلًا سَلَامًا سَلَامًا (26)

They will not hear therein any idle talk or sinful speech (25) except the words of peace, peace (26)

Section Four Key

■ **Verse 16-17 worksheet**

1.   Allah سبحانه وتعالى is warning us about case number three.
2.   In verse number (17) Allah ALL Mighty states to us clearly that: the hereafter is better and more lasting. وَالْأَخِرَةُ خَيْرٌ وَأَبْقَى

■ **Verse number (18) worksheet**

II.   إِنَّ هَذَا لَفِي الصُّحُفِ الْأُولَى

■ **Verse number (19) worksheet (B)**

1.   Adam (PBUH)
2.   Muhammad (PBUH)
3.   Musa and Ibrahim (PBUT)
4.   Allah سبحانه وتعالى has given us guidance that is suitable and helpful to all humans throughout history and until the end of time. The message of mono theism is the same to ALL mankind. Allah also in many places of the Holy Quran has explained to us that this life on Earth is temporary. We should believe in our only creator Allah and use our time here to perform deeds that are going to help us go to Paradise.

■ **Section (4) review worksheet (A)**

ق	ا	خ	ف	ح	ص	ل	ا
ى	ل	و	أ	ل	ا	ث	خ
ى	د	ن	و	ر	ث	ؤ	ت
س	ن	ا	ل	أ	خ	ر	ه
و	ي	ر	ى	ق	ب	أ	ن
م	ا	ب	ص	م	ر	ي	خ

■ **Section (4) review worksheet (B)**

1	2	3	4
D	G	H	C
5	6	7	8
E	B	A	F

■ **Section (4) review worksheet (C)**

بَلْ تُؤْثِرُونَ ٱلْحَيَوٰةَ ٱلدُّنْيَا (16) وَٱلْأَخِرَةُ خَيْرٌ وَ أَبْقَىٰ (17) إِنَّ هَٰذَا لَفِي ٱلصُّحُفِ ٱلْأُولَىٰ (18) صُحُفِ إِبْرَٰهِيمَ وَمُوسَىٰ (19)

End of chapter
Self Reflections

My favourite verse is ...... because ....

Currently during this time in my life i can relate to verse number ...... because ....

Verse number ..... reminds me of ....

I can implement verse number .... by doing the following ....

Chapter 89 take away points \ personal lessons learned ......

The Most High

Board Game

Board Game Rules
Number of Players: 2-4

Goal
The aim of this game is to review Surat AL-A'la and be the first to reach the **FINISH** point.

Materials Included:
1. Board
2. Questions
   (Cut & separate into 48 game cards)

Materials Needed:
1. Game pieces or pawns (1 per group)
   (can use different color clothes buttons)
2. Six-sided Dice (1 per group)

I.   Cut & separate questions into 48 game cards. Place ALL cards upsides down on one side of the board (the cards are shuffled before the beginning of each game).

II.   Each team will roll the dice to determine the order of the game. The team with the highest number will go first (team A) and the team with the lowest number will go second (team B).

1. **2 teams** play against each other **(A & B)**
2. First question is read by **team B** member.
3. Only one **team A** member answers the question (selected member rotates).
4. If **team A** answers question correctly, they roll the dice and move the team marker accordingly.
5. If **team A** doesn't answer question correctly, the **team A** marker stays in place and the dice is not rolled.
6. The next question is read by **team A** member for the second round of play. If **team B** answers correctly then they roll the dice and move their marker accordingly; and if they answer incorrectly, they don't roll the dice or move their marker.
7. Both teams take turns answering the questions and rolling the dice.
8. Any team can take advantage of the short cuts when their marker lands on a short cut point.
9. The game continues in the same way until the **FINISH** point is reached.
10. The team that reaches the **FINISH** point first wins.

Start

1
2
3
4
5
6
7
8
9
10
11
12
13
14
15
16
17
18
19
20
21
22
23
24
25
26
27
28
29
30
31
32
33
34
35
36
37
38
39

Finish

Shortcut

Shortcut

Shortcut

Board Game Questions

What is the Quranic word that means the Most High?

Answer: الأَعْلَى

Recite the first 5 verses of Surat الأَعْلَى

From: سَبِّح ....

Recite the verse that is translated as follows: "and who brings forth the pasture"

Answer: Verse (4)

What is the opposite of the Quranic word يَمُوتُ

Answer: يَحْيَى

What is the Quranic word that means The Great Fire?

Answer: النَّارَالكُبْرَى

What is the name of the book that Allah revealed to Prophet Musa (PBUH)

Answer: The Torah التَّوْرَاة

Unscramble the following words from verse 9:

نفعت / إن / فذكر / الذكرى

Answer:

فذَكِّر إن نفعت الذكرى

Give four examples of remembrance (things we say)?

Answer:

الحمد لله، الله أكبر، سبحان الله
استغفر الله، لا إله إلا الله

According to the Quran, the hereafter is ....
a) better   b) more lasting
c) temporary
d) a and b are the correct answers

Answer: d

What is the Quranic word that means The former scriptures?

Answer: الصُّحُفِ الأُولى

Fill in the blank:
We will teach you the _____ ,so you will not forget.

Answer: Quran

Recite the verse that is translated as follows: "Indeed,he who purifies himself will attain success"

Answer: Verse (14)

The Quranic word سَبِّح **in verse one means**
a) remind   b) glorify
c) take heed   d) created

Answer: b

Unscramble the following words from verse 16:
الدنيا / بل / الحياة / تؤثرون

Answer:
بَلْ تُؤْثِرُونَ الْحَيَاةَ الدُّنْيَا

What is the opposite of the Quranic word الْجَهْرَ

Answer: مَا يَخْفَي

The Quranic word هَدَى **in verse 3 means:**
a) easy way   b) attain Success
c) hereafter   d) inspired

Answer: d

The Arabic word دِرْهَم **means :**
a) Silver Coin   b) Gold Coin
c) Black-boarded Cloak
d) None of the above.

Answer: a

The Quranic word فَلَا تَنْسَى **in verse 6 means:**
a) pasture   b) nor live
c) nor die   d) so you will not forget

Answer: d

Unscramble the following words from verse 14:

أفلح / تزكى / قد / من

Answer: قَدْ أَفْلَحَ مَنْ تَزَكَّى

According to the Quran, the wretched is someone who....

a) has no money   b) is unlucky

c) takes the easy way to heaven

d) avoids the reminders

Answer: d

Finish reciting verse (7):

إلا مَا ....

Answer:

إلا ما شَاء الله إنه يَعلَمُ الجَهرَ
وَمَا يخْفَى

The Quranic word أَحْوَى **in verse 5 means:**

a) Black/dark   b) Green

c) what is hudden   d) more lasting

Answer: a

Fill in the missing Quranic word from verse 11:

وَيَتَجَنَّبُهَا ....

What does it mean?

Answer:

The wretched الأَشْقَى

The Quranic word مَا يَخْفَى **in verse 7 means**

a) reminder   b) glorify

c) what is hidden d) take heed

Answer: c

Who is the last of the prophets?

Answer: Muhammad

عليه الصلاة والسلام

Recite the last 4 verses of Surat الأَعْلَى

from: بَلْ ....

The Arabic word خَمِيصَه **means   :**

a) Silver Coin   b) Gold Coin

c) Black-boarded Cloak

d) None of the above.

Answer: c

The Quranic word الأَخِرَة **in verse 17 means:**

a) paradise   b) attain Success

c) hereafter   d) more lasting

Answer: c

What is the Quranic word that means created?s

Answer: خَلَقَ

Unscramble the following words from verse 2 :

فَ / خلق / سوى/ الذي

Answer: الَّذِي خَلَقَ فَسَوَّىٰ

Recite the verse that is translated as follows: "We will guide you to the easy way"

Answer: Verse (8)

وَنُيَسِّرُكَ لِلْيُسْرَىٰ

Recite the verse that is translated as follows: "wherein he will neither die nor live"

Answer: ثُمَّ لَا يَمُوتُ فِيهَا وَلَا يَحْيَىٰ

Verse 13

Unscramble the following words from verse one :

الأعلى / ربك / سبح / اسم

Answer:

سَبِّحِ اسْمَ رَبِّكَ الْأَعْلَى

Recite the verse that is translated as follows: "and who determined [the creation] then inspired them"

Answer: وَالَّذِي قَدَّرَ فَهَدَىٰ

Verse 3

The Quranic word الذِّكْرَىٰ in verse 9 means :

a) reminder   b) glorify

c) nor die   d) take heed

Answer: a

What are the creations that Allah made with his own hands?

Answer:
1. The pen 2. His Thrown
3. The Garden of Eden and
4. Our father Adam (PBUH)

Fill in the missing Quranic word from verse 8:

وَنُيَسِّرُكَ ....

What does it mean?

Answer:

The easy way لِلْيُسْرَىٰ

The language of the Holy Quran is..

a) unique   b) poetic

c) rhymes

d) All of the above except b

Answer: a

The Arabic word دِينَار means
a) Silver Coin   b) Gold Coin
c) Black-boarded Cloak
d) None of the above

Answer: b

The Quranic word تُؤْثِرُون in verse 16 means
a) inspired   b) nor live
c) prefer   d) more lasting

Answer: c

Unscramble the following words from verse 18 :
هذا / الصحف/ لفي/الأولى/ إن

Answer:
إِنَّ هَذَا لَفِي الصُّحُفِ الْأُولَى

What is the creation that was used in this workbook to explain verse (3)
وَالَّذِي قَدَّرَ فَهَدَى ?
a) ants   b) flowers
c) honeybees   d) pasture

Answer: c

Who is the father of the prophets?

Answer:
Prophet Ibrahim
عليه السلام

The Quranic word مَا يَخْفَى in verse 7 means
a) reminder   b) glorify
c) what is hidden d) take heed

Answer: c

Why did Allah talk about
the green pasture and then in the next verse talk about the black dead pasture?
Answer: As a proof of his ability and to remind us that everything has an ending.

The Quranic word أَفْلَحَ in verse 14 means:
a) paradise   b) attain Success
c) created   d) more lasting

Answer: b

According to the Quran, our preference is the ....
a) hereafter   b) the worldly life
c) more lasting way
d) a and b are the correct answers

Answer: b

Fill in the missing Quranic word from verse 4:
وَالَّذِي أَخْرَجَ الْمَرْعَى ....
What does it mean?

Answer: الْمَرْعَى **Pasture**

The Most High

Book Review

Praise be to Allah for leading me to review this invaluable workbook. A unique and simplified approach to the study and memorization of Quran Chapter 87.

What sets this book apart is its ability to guide the students through the intricate process of committing the verses to memory with remarkable ease. The author's skillful presentation ensures that the memorization transcends mere rote learning, providing a profound understanding of the meanings encapsulated within the Quranic chapter 87. The workbook goes beyond the surface, unraveling the layers of meanings woven into the verses, allowing the reader to embark on a journey of comprehension and reflection. Many activities and exercises transform the study of the verses to a journey of spiritual growth.

One noteworthy feature that further enhances the book's utility is its inclusion of lessons on writing and copying Quranic vocabulary. This hands-on dimension adds a valuable component to the learning process, enabling students to engage with the written form of the sacred words they are committing to memory. The holistic approach of combining memorization with the text and the ability to write and copy Quranic vocabulary fosters a comprehensive learning experience.

I wholeheartedly recommend this workbook to anyone seeking to learn Quran Chapter 87. Whether you are a seasoned student of Islamic studies or a beginner taking the first steps on this spiritual path, the benefits derived from this workbook are boundless. May Allah continue to bless the efforts of those involved in producing such impactful works, serving as a means of guidance and enlightenment for generations to come.

Shaykha Ebtsam Fawzy